Farewell to
STEAM

ROGER SIVITER
ARPS

SUTTON PUBLISHING

First published in 2004 by
Sutton Publishing, an imprint of NPI Media Group
Cirencester Road · Chalford · Stroud · Gloucestershire · GL6 8PE

Reprinted 2007

British Library Cataloguing in Publication Data
A catalogue record for this book is available from the British Library.

ISBN 978-0-7509-3500-5

On Saturday 30 July 1966, ex-LMS Class 5MT 4–6–0 No. 45402 speeds over Lea
water troughs near Salwick on the Blackpool–Preston line with a mid-morning
Blackpool–Manchester train. Note the 10D shed-plate – Lostock Hall shed, Preston.
This shed remained open until the very end of BR steam, on 11 August 1968.

Typeset in 10/12 pt Palatino.
Typesetting and origination by
Sutton Publishing.
Printed and bound in England.

Contents

Ex-LMS 'Black Five' 4–6–0 No. 45345 receives attention at the southern end of Preston station before leaving with the 17.52 train to Liverpool on Sunday 25 February 1968.

Introduction

This book covers the last three years of BR steam working, from the summer of 1965 to the '15 Guinea Special' of 11 August 1968. This was certainly not the glamour period of BR steam; without doubt, that was the 1950s, when Britain's railways were back in full swing after the Second World War and the restraints that had followed in the immediate postwar years.

By the middle of 1965, steam haulage was confined to a limited number of areas. Many parts of the country were already dieselised, notably whole areas of the South-East, South-West and Eastern England, parts of Wales and many areas of Scotland. Also by that time, whole classes of locomotive had been withdrawn from service and scrapped, and many locomotives had had their name-plates removed, as well as the cabside number-plates on ex-GWR locomotives. Most locomotives looked the worse for wear, yet many were in good mechanical order and well capable of the many duties still required of them, this being in no small way due to the top-class locomotive shed staff who maintained them, and the footplate crews who could still coax the best out of their charges.

Perhaps therein lies the fascination of this period in the history of the British steam locomotive. There were still many locomotives and areas to photograph, but enthusiasts knew the end was nearly nigh. And so people would travel great distances to photograph the last of a certain class of locomotive at work, or the last steam workings on a particular line.

It was all good fun and many friendships were formed. I am pleased to say that I still see many friends on the lineside today whom I first met in the final years of BR steam.

In compiling this book I am grateful to the many BR men who made it possible; to photographers Ben Ashworth, Hugh Ballantyne, John Cooper-Smith, Ken Hale and Michael Mensing, who allowed me to choose from their collections; and to my wife Christina for typing the manuscript.

Unless otherwise specified, all photographs were taken by the author.

Roger Siviter ARPS
Evesham, 2004

Former GWR Class 5700 0–6–0 pannier tank No. 3619 disappears into Old Hill tunnel (on the Kidderminster–Birmingham Snow Hill line) as it banks a heavy Halesowen to Bordesley goods up Old Hill bank on the early evening of Monday 22 August 1966. The train locomotive is No. 3609 of the same class.

Chapter One

South & West

The Southern Region line from Waterloo to Southampton, Bournemouth and Weymouth provided the last steam workings into the nation's capital. At midday on Monday 5 June 1967 (within a few weeks of the end of steam on 9 July) former Southern Railway rebuilt 'West Country' Pacific locomotive No. 34090 (formerly named *Sir Eustace Missenden, Southern Railway*) is seen at Waterloo station after arrival with an Up Bournemouth train.

Right until the end of steam on the Southern Region, Nine Elms shed (70A) had an allocation of BR Standard Class 4MT 2–6–4 tanks for shunting and trip working. No. 80015 is seen at Waterloo station on 5 June 1967 with the empty coaching stock of the train seen in the previous picture. This locomotive was built in 1951 and would be withdrawn within a few weeks of this photograph being taken.

Ex-SR unrebuilt 'West Country' Pacific No. 34102 *Lapford* passes Surbiton on 30 June 1966 with the 13.30 Waterloo to Bournemouth train. These lightweight 4–6–2s were introduced in 1945 and designed by O.V. Bulleid, primarily for work on the Southern Railway's West Country routes. (*John Cooper-Smith*)

The classic Southern scene, as rebuilt 'West Country' Pacific No. 34100 *Appledore*, with the Down 'Bournemouth Belle' all-Pullman train (12.30 ex-Waterloo), runs through New Malden on 18 August 1966. This train made its final run on 9 July 1967, still locomotive-hauled, albeit with diesel traction in charge in the shape of Brush Type 4 diesel No. D1924, steam traction having finished on 29 December 1966. No. 34100 was built in 1949, rebuilt in 1960 and withdrawn in July 1967. (*John Cooper-Smith*)

Rebuilt 'Battle of Britain' 4–6–2 No. 34060 *25 Squadron* is caught by the camera as it heads towards London on Saturday 10 September 1966 with the 13.25 Weymouth–Waterloo train. The location is the former LSWR four-track section at Deep Cut, near Pirbright.

On Good Friday 1966 (8 April), rebuilt 'West Country' Pacific No. 34034 (formerly *Honiton*) runs through Basing, to the east of Basingstoke, with the midday Waterloo–Bournemouth train. By this time, many of the Southern 4–6–2s were beginning to lose their name-plates and crests.

Steam on the Southern finished on 9 July 1967, the electrified route between Waterloo and Bournemouth opening the following day. The final steam working into Waterloo was the 14.07 from Weymouth, hauled by 'Merchant Navy' Pacific No. 35030 (formerly *Elder Dempster Lines*). To mark the end of steam, the Southern Region ran two special trains on Sunday 2 July 1967 from Waterloo to Bournemouth. The second of these two 'Farewell to Steam' specials is seen on the outward journey near Basing, hauled by 'Merchant Navy' Pacific No. 35028 *Clan Line*, now happily preserved. The second picture shows the first special train as it leaves Basingstoke on its return journey, with 'Merchant Navy' 4–6–2 No. 35008 *Orient Line* in charge.

Also on 2 July 1967, 'West Country' Pacific No. 34025 (formerly *Whimple*) is seen near Worting Junction with a morning Waterloo–Bournemouth service train.

A wet Maundy Thursday 1966 (7 April) at Basingstoke station, as unrebuilt 'Battle of Britain' 4–6–2 No. 34064 *Fighter Command* approaches platform one with a Waterloo–Salisbury stopping train. Steam workings west of Salisbury had more or less finished with the advent of the 1965 summer timetable, but Salisbury shed (72B) would remain open until the end of Southern steam. However, No. 34064 had only a few more weeks of service, being withdrawn on 22 May 1966.

This view, also taken at Basingstoke on the same day as the previous photograph, shows grimy BR Standard Class 5MT 4–6–0 No. 73085 about to depart with the 17.37 to Woking. Note the magnificent Southern Railway gantry signal and the SR station lamps. The line to Reading can also be seen (in the middle of the gantry) curving away to the left.

We leave the Bournemouth line and travel down to Guildford, where, on 8 June 1966, the very last Maunsell Class N and U 2–6–0s were to be seen still in steam. Class N No. 31408 pulls away from the coaling plant where Class U No. 31639 is still being coaled. I was very lucky to capture on film these last two locomotives, because they had officially been taken out of service on 5 June and were withdrawn shortly after these photographs were taken. Although very similar in appearance, the N Class is a more powerful locomotive, with a tractive effort of 26,035lb, compared to the 23,865lb of the U Class.

In January 1966, the Locomotive Club of Great Britain ran two S15 commemorative tours, from Waterloo to Eastleigh works via the Alton line, and also the Bentley–Bordon branch with U Class 2–6–0 No. 31639 (see opposite below). Originally, just one trip was planned, for Sunday 16 January, but such was the demand for tickets that another trip was run on the Sunday before (9 January). The outward trip on 9 January is seen climbing Medstead bank on the single-line section between Alton and Alresford, with ex-SR Class S15 4–6–0 No. 30837 in charge. This locomotive was one of a batch built by the Southern Railway between 1927 and 1936, to a design by Maunsell. (*Ken Hale*)

Our next location is the deep chalk cutting just north of Waller's Ash tunnel, situated between Micheldever and Winchester on the Basingstoke and Southampton–Bournemouth line. Rebuilt 'Merchant Navy' Pacific No. 35024 *East Asiatic Company* is seen heading towards Southampton on Saturday 23 July 1966 with the midday train from Waterloo.

Eastleigh was not only home to one of the Southern Railway's works but also a locomotive shed – No. 70D. Photographed inside the shed on Sunday 21 August 1966 is an unidentified 'West Country' Pacific locomotive, behind which is USA 0–6–0 tank No. 30073. These locomotives were bought by the SR from the US Army in 1946, and were then fitted with a modified cab and bunker, and other detail alterations. (*B.J. Ashworth*)

This scene, photographed on 30 December 1966, shows Southampton Central station in transition under rebuilding. Rebuilt 'Battle of Britain' 4–6–2 No. 34071 *601 Squadron*, leaking steam on a cold winter's morning, stands with the 09.24 Bournemouth–Waterloo service. On the left is BR Standard 5MT 4–6–0 No. 73087. (*Hugh Ballantyne*)

After leaving Southampton, the line to Bournemouth runs through the New Forest, and a mile to the south-west of Brockenhurst (in the heart of the New Forest) lies Lymington Junction, junction for the short branch to the Hampshire holiday and yachting resort of Lymington, which is also a ferry port for the Isle of Wight. BR Standard Class 4 2–6–4 tank No. 80139 approaches Lymington Junction on the misty evening of 20 July 1966 with a Brockenhurst–Lymington branch train. The branch can be seen curving away to the left by the junction signal-box.

The Lymington branch had the distinction of being the last steam-worked branch line in the country, steam finishing here on 2 April 1967. A few days before the end of steam, on 11 March 1967, Standard Class 4 2–6–4 tank No. 80152 makes a fine sight as it heads through the wooded section of the line just north of Lymington with a train for Brockenhurst. The locomotive had been specially cleaned by the photographer and other members of the Master Neverers' Association (MNA). This group of young men, of whom Ken Hale was one of the leading lights, would often spend hours cleaning locomotives in order to get the 'master shot', and it certainly paid off, as can be seen in this lovely photograph. (*Ken Hale*)

While staying at Lymington in July 1966, the author took a day trip to the Isle of Wight, travelling on the ferry from Lymington to Yarmouth. By 1966, the lines on the Isle of Wight had been cut back to just one between Ryde and Shanklin. However, steam was still in charge, in the shape of the delightful former LSWR Class 02 0–4–4 tank locomotives, designed by Adams and introduced in 1889. Their reign would end by 31 December 1966, when their duties would be taken over by London Transport tube trains. These four pictures were all taken on Thursday 21 July 1966 and show, top left, No. 33 *Bembridge* as it heads across Ryde pier with a midday train from Shanklin. In the foreground are the lines of the pier tramway. The second view shows No. 33 again, this time near Whitefield Woods, between St Johns and Brading, with the 11.10 Ryde–Shanklin train. Note the Westinghouse brake, which was fitted in 1923. Above, No. 28 *Ashey* is seen on the double-track section just south of St Johns with a morning Shanklin–Ryde train. The Victorian rolling stock complements this vintage scene. The final picture in this 'Island Quartet' was taken south of Brading, and shows the 14.25 Ryde–Shanklin train with No. 16 *Ventnor* in charge. I mentioned that all the other lines on the Isle of Wight had closed by 1965. However, the line from Wootton to Havenstreet and Smallbrook Junction has happily been preserved, with trains now running between March and October.

We leave the Isle of Wight and return to the Bournemouth–Weymouth line, just to the west of Lymington Junction, where, on the late evening of Wednesday 20 July 1966, BR Standard Class 4 4–6–0 No. 75068 hurries through the gloom with a Southampton–Bournemouth passenger train.

The following evening (after my day trip to the Isle of Wight), the weather was much better, and I was able to photograph a late-evening (around 8p.m.) Brockenhurst–Lymington train, hauled by ex-LMS Class 2MT 2–6–2 tank No. 41316. This picture was taken from roughly the same location as the previous one.

On the next evening (22 July), still at the same location, we first of all see ex-SR rebuilt 'West Country' Pacific No. 34001 (formerly *Exeter*) as it heads for Bournemouth with a tea-time train from Waterloo. This locomotive was the first of the class to be built, having entered service in May 1945. It was rebuilt in 1957 and withdrawn at the end of Southern Region steam in July 1967. The second view, taken a few minutes earlier, shows another member of this handsome class, No. 34037 *Clovelly*, as it hurries away from the camera with a Bournemouth–Waterloo express. Note the SR platelayers' hut of concrete construction.

After Bournemouth, the line to Weymouth skirts Poole Harbour, where, on 22 July 1966, BR Standard Class 4 2–6–0 No. 76014 is seen near Holes Bay Junction with an afternoon Weymouth–Bournemouth local. Holes Bay was the junction for the line to Broadstone and then on to the Somerset & Dorset Joint line to Templecombe and Bath, which sadly had closed in the previous March. Note the assortment of lineside huts.

A mile or so to the west of Wareham is Worgret Junction, which is the junction for the branch line to Swanage. Ex-LMS Class 2MT 2–6–2 tank No. 41230 leaves the station at Corfe Castle with the 13.28 Swanage–Wareham train on 22 July 1966. This line closed in January 1972, but happily part of the line has been preserved and is now known as the Swanage Railway, with trains running between Swanage and Norden Park-and-Ride.

At the Dorset county town of Dorchester, the SR line from Bournemouth joins the GWR route from Yeovil and Westbury for the run down to the south coast resort and ferry port of Weymouth. On Sunday 4 June 1967, a Weymouth–Southampton freight approaches Dorchester West station, hauled by a typical motive power combination of the time – diesel and steam. Type 3 Birmingham RC&W 1550hp BoBo diesel-electric (later Class 33) No. D6569 pilots BR Standard Class 4 4–6–0 No. 75074. (*Michael Mensing*)

Sunday 21 August 1966 sees a variety of locomotives at Weymouth shed (71G), including ex-SR rebuilt 4–6–2 No. 35029 *Ellerman Lines* and BR Standard Class 4MT 2–6–0 No. 76033. Also on shed are a mixture of unidentified BR Standard Class locomotives and ex-SR Pacifics. This shed, which closed in July 1967, was situated on the east side of the line, north of Weymouth station. (*B.J. Ashworth*)

The Waterloo–Exeter trains, apart from diesel failures, had finished with steam traction from the start of the summer timetable of 1965. However, Salisbury shed (70E) continued to have an allocation of locomotives until the end of Southern Region steam. These would work some passenger turns to Basingstoke and Waterloo, as well as numerous freight workings. Early on a misty spring morning, 7 April 1966, BR Standard Class 4 4–6–0 No. 75074 (shedded at Eastleigh) receives attention in the shed yard before leaving with a freight for the Southampton area. Through the mist on the left-hand side can be seen the medieval spire of Salisbury Cathedral – the tallest in Europe at 400ft.

After the end of regular steam workings on the Southern Region's Exeter route, several special charter trains were run between Waterloo and Devon's second city. In March 1966, ex-LNER A4 Pacific No. 60024 *Kingfisher* came down to Nine Elms from Aberdeen to work two Southern Region tours. Here, on 27 March, the A4 heads west near the closed halt at Sutton Bingham (just west of Yeovil Junction) with a Waterloo–Exeter special train, organised by the Locomotive Club of Great Britain (LCGB). The previous day, No. 60024 had worked a special train from Waterloo to Bournemouth and Weymouth for the A4 Preservation Society. (*Hugh Ballantyne*)

On August bank holiday, 30 August 1965, BR Standard Class 4 2–6–0 No. 76013 climbs out of Bath (S&DJR) with the 17.55 Bristol–Bournemouth West train. The location is where the S&D line crosses over the former GWR main line to Bristol. (*Michael Mensing*)

Just over six months after the previous photograph, on the weekend of 5/6 March 1966, the last rites on the S&D were taking place. On Saturday 5 March 1966, the last public service day on the line, BR Standard Class 4 2–6–4 tank No. 80043, driven by Cecil Waldron, leaves Wellow with the 16.25 Bath Green Park to Templecombe. This was the last service train to leave Bath in daylight, and was also the penultimate departure. (*Hugh Ballantyne*)

Also on 5 March 1966 were two special 'farewell' trains, run by the Great Western Society and the LCGB respectively. The LCGB special, hauled by a pair of ex-SR unrebuilt Pacifics, ran from Bournemouth to Evercreech Junction, where two Class 2MT tanks, Nos 41307 and 41249, took over for a return trip down the Highbridge branch. The branch special is seen here near Glastonbury on the outward journey. (*Ken Hale*)

After returning to Evercreech Junction from the trip to Highbridge, the special then ran to Bath with the immaculate-looking No. 34006 *Bude* and No. 34057 *Biggin Hill* now in charge. The special is seen pausing at Chilcompton en route to Bath. Two more special trains were run on the following day (6 March). Then, sadly, the line was closed and lifted. (*Hugh Ballantyne*)

Opposite, top: When this photograph of Bristol Bath Road shed (82A) open day was taken on 23 October 1965, very little steam activity remained in the Bristol area, and it had ceased altogether by the end of that year. Everyone seems to be having a great time looking around the wide variety of steam locomotives and diesel traction on display. I wonder what those lads can see looking down the chimney of the pannier tank. Happy days! In 1954 a couple of Army pals and I were travelling overnight from the Salisbury area to Birmingham via Bristol for a short leave (we had been playing on a gig at Andover with the Worcesters' regimental dance band) when we fell asleep before reaching Bristol, only to be awakened at around 6a.m. in the carriage sidings by the cleaning staff who – seeing that we were 'squaddies' – arranged for us to have a lift to Temple Meads station on the footplate of a 'Castle' locomotive, a most exciting journey of a few hundred yards. To follow that, we rode behind an ex-LMS 'Jubilee' 4–6–0 on the Birmingham train, which included being banked up the Lickey incline by 'Big Bertha', the ex-MR 0–10–0 No. 58100. (*B.J. Ashworth*)

Opposite, bottom: Moving north to Gloucester, where steam finished on 1 January 1966 with the closure to steam of Horton Road shed (85B), we see the last active 'Castle' Class 4–6–0, No. 7029 *Clun Castle*, receiving attention on 15 October 1965. 'Modified Hall' Class 4–6–0 No. 7927 *Willington Hall* is in the background being turned. Also, on the left-hand side of the picture can be seen Gloucester Eastgate station, which closed in 1975. (*B.J. Ashworth*)

A few days later, on 30 October 1965, 'Modified Hall' Class 4–6–0 No. 7914 (formerly *Lleweni Hall*) heads past Horton Road shed towards Gloucester Central station. (*B.J. Ashworth*)

Gloucester Central station is the last location in this section, and this view shows ex-GW 'Manor' Class 4–6–0 No. 7829 *Ramsbury Manor* waiting to leave with the 17.00 Gloucester–Cheltenham St James train on 6 November 1965. No. 7829, together with No. 7808 *Cookham Manor*, were the last of the class to be withdrawn in December 1965. However, No. 7808, unlike No. 7829, survives into preservation, together with several other examples of this famous class. (*B.J. Ashworth*)

Chapter Two
Wales & the Borders

On the Welsh border, at the ancient Shropshire county town of Shrewsbury, steam remained active until the end of the through working from Paddington to Chester on 4 March 1967. On a sunny 23 April 1966, BR Standard Class 4MT 4–6–0 No. 75012 departs for Machynlleth and Aberystwyth/Barmouth with the Down 'Cambrian Coast Express', the Paddington–Shrewsbury section having been worked by a Class 47 diesel.

By the latter half of 1965, steam had virtually finished in South and West Wales and between Newport and Shrewsbury, and the scrapyards – particularly Woodham's at Barry – were fast filling up with locomotives from the area and further afield. A visit to Barry on 8 May 1966 shows ex-SR U Class 2–6–0 No. 31618 and the rear of ex-GWR Class 4200 2–8–0 tank No. 4277. On the same day at Cashmore's scrapyard at Newport, BR Standard Class 3MT 2–6–2 tank No. 82041 is seen in front of an unidentified ex-GWR Class 41XX 2–6–2 tank. No. 82041 had been withdrawn in December 1965, its final shed being Bath Green Park (82F).

This photograph was taken in the Forest of Dean on the borders of Gloucestershire and Wales at Northern United colliery, on 19 August 1965. Ex-GWR Class 5700 0–6–0 pannier tank No. 4689 is seen shunting empty wagons. This colliery, the last NCB mine in the Forest of Dean, was closed by the following Christmas. (*B.J. Ashworth*)

The end of steam on the Cambrian route, as 4–6–0 No. 75033 climbs up the 1 in 52 of Talerddig bank with the Up Cambrian Coast Express on Saturday 4 March 1967, the final day of the through workings from Paddington. Judging by the immaculate state of the locomotive, it looks as though the 'Neverers' have been at work again. Note also the headboard. (*Ken Hale*)

Opposite: On 27 August 1966, a pair of BR Standard Class 4MT Moguls, Nos 76038 and 76047, climb the 1 in 52 of Talerddig bank in mid-Wales with the 10.30 Pwllheli–Birmingham train. This class of 2–6–0 locomotive was first introduced in December 1952, being built at both Horwich and Doncaster works. All were withdrawn by the end of 1967, but happily several examples survived into preservation. The previous Saturday (20 August) the 10.30 ex-Pwllheli was hauled by a pair of BR Standard Class 4MT 4–6–0s, Nos 75055 and 75060, seen approaching the summit of Talerddig bank in fine style. Several members of this class were active until the end of steam in August 1968 and, like the 2–6–0s, some examples were preserved.

To mark the end of the through workings on the Paddington–Chester–Birkenhead route, several special trains were run over the weekend of 4/5 March 1967. On Saturday 4 March, two special trains were run from Paddington to Birkenhead, organised by Ian Allan. The second of these two special charters, the 'Birkenhead Flyer', hauled by GWR 'Castle' Class 4–6–0 No. 4079 *Pendennis Castle*, is seen heading north off the Dee viaduct (just south of Ruabon) on its outward journey. No. 4079, after a long sojourn in Australia, is now back in the UK at the Great Western Society headquarters at Didcot. (*Ken Hale*)

Opposite, top: Moving on to the Shrewsbury–Chester line, we see Standard Class 4MT 4–6–0 No. 75046 near Trehowell, heading south towards Gobowen with an empty ballast train for Blodwell Quarry, some 5 miles south of Oswestry on the old Cambrian line from Gobowen, on 2 August 1966.

Opposite, bottom: In many ways, this book is often about 'the last of the class'. This was certainly the case with the ex-GWR Class 5600 0–6–2 tank. The last two of the class, Nos 5605 and 6697, were both shedded at Croes Newydd shed (formerly 89B, then 6C in LM days), Wrexham. This picture was taken at Wrexham on 19 May 1966 and shows No. 6697 shunting coal wagons in the yard. A few days later, both locomotives were withdrawn. Happily, No. 6697 is preserved by the GW Society at Didcot. These sturdy tank locomotives were designed by Collett for service in the Welsh valleys, and were introduced in 1924. They were equally at home on freight or local passenger workings.

Croes Newydd shed at Wrexham also provided the locomotives that worked the Brymbo colliery and Minera limestone works branch line, situated to the north-west of Wrexham. On 22 April 1967, ex-LMS Class 4MT 2–6–0 No. 43088 is seen at Brymbo North with the Tuesdays/Thursdays/Saturdays-only 08.25 Croes Newydd yard to Minera limestone works empties. Croes Newydd shed (6C), along with Chester shed (6A) (see opposite above), was closed to steam on 5 June 1967. (*Ken Hale*)

Ex-LMS Hughes/Fowler Class 5MT 2–6–0 No. 42942 pauses at Chester General station on 17 October 1966, before proceeding to Birkenhead and its home shed (8H). No. 42942 was one of the last of this popular class, which were affectionately known as 'Crabs', and was withdrawn by January 1967.

A visit to Chester shed (6A) on Sunday 24 April 1966 shows BR Standard Class 4MT 2–6–0 No. 76095, behind which is ex-LMS Class 5MT 4–6–0 No. 45350, and on the left-hand side the shed yard 'goat', ex-LMS Class 3F 0–6–0 tank No. 47437. These tank locomotives were known as 'Jinties' and were part of a post-Grouping development of a Midland Railway design. They were introduced in 1924.

The line from Chester to Birkenhead via Hooton still saw steam activity in 1966, and on 23 August of that year, BR Class 9F 2–10–0 No. 92159 heads north through the former station of Mollington (which closed in 1960) with an afternoon mixed-goods train bound for Birkenhead. At the rear of the train can be seen the small goods yard, which at the time was still in use as an oil terminal.

Another 'Wirral' freight, this time just south of Hooton. Our old friend 'Crab' 2–6–0 No. 42942 makes a handsome sight as it heads for Chester with a tank train from Ellesmere Port on 10 December 1966. The locomotive looks in fine fettle, courtesy of the 'Neverers'. (*Ken Hale*)

Steam on some of the Chester–Birkenhead services lasted until March 1967. On 20 August 1966, ex-LMS Stanier Class 4MT 2–6–4 tank No. 42613 pulls out of Hooton station with the 14.45 Birkenhead–Paddington express (note the Class A express lamps). The big 2–6–4 tank will work the train only up to Chester, where diesel traction will take over. (*Hugh Ballantyne*)

We leave the Wirral area and head for North Wales, where the former LNWR main line to Holyhead still saw steam activity in 1966. These two views, taken on 8 September 1966, show BR 'Britannia' Class Pacific No. 70032 *Tennyson* approaching the medieval town of Conway with an afternoon Holyhead–Crewe parcels train. These handsome 4–6–2s were first introduced in 1951, No. 70032 being withdrawn in September 1967.

Several of the Holyhead–Bangor–Manchester Victoria passenger trains were still steam-worked in 1966, mainly by BR Standard Class 5MT 4–6–0s off Manchester Patricroft shed (9H). One of Patricroft's 4–6–0s, No. 73033, glints in the late sunlight as it heads past Penmaenmawr on the North Wales coast with an evening Bangor–Manchester train on 7 September 1966.

Our final photograph in North Wales was taken on the evening of 6 September 1966, and shows ex-LMS Class 5MT 4–6–0 No. 45116 taking water at Llandudno Junction station, prior to leaving with a Holyhead–Broad Street (London) goods train. Note the container on the open wagon, providing businesses with a 'door-to-door' service.

Chapter Three

The Midlands

Steam traction survived well into the spring of 1967 in the Midlands. However, one unique working in the East Midlands that finished in the latter half of 1965 was the Seaton Junction–Stamford steam-hauled push-and-pull train. This photograph was taken in June 1965 and shows BR Standard Class 2MT 2–6–2 tank No. 84008 leaving Seaton Junction for Stamford with a push-and-pull service. Only thirty of these small 2–6–2 tanks were built, being first introduced in 1953. No. 84008 was withdrawn in October 1965, its final shed being Leicester (15A). (*John Cooper-Smith*)

Another East Midlands scene, this time south of Loughborough on the Midland main line to Leicester and St Pancras. On 22 August 1965, ex-LMS Stanier Class 8F 2–8–0 No. 48349 blackens the sky as it hurries south with a heavy mixed-freight train. (*John Cooper-Smith*)

The last day of the through workings on the GCR (3 September 1966) sees the 17.15 Nottingham Victoria–Marylebone train passing the site of Culworth station, hauled by Stanier Class 5 4–6–0 No. 44984. This site is just 3 miles south of Woodford Halse and 1 mile south of Culworth Junction, which was the junction for the line to Banbury. Note the symbolic wreath on the smokebox door. (*Michael Mensing*)

The GCR through workings between Nottingham Victoria and Marylebone finished on 3 September 1966 (see p. 44, bottom) and were steam-worked right until the end. In June 1965, 'Black Five' 4–6–0 No. 44920 is pictured leaving Loughborough (GC) with a Nottingham–Marylebone train. (*John Cooper-Smith*)

These two views were taken on Thursday 1 September 1966 at Nottingham Victoria station. 'Black Five' No. 44984 is seen again as it works light out of Mansfield Road tunnel and is about to pass the elegant former GCR Victoria North signal-box. A few minutes later, Class 8F 2–8–0 No. 48510 pulls through the south end of Victoria station with an Up coal train. This spacious station was opened in 1900, and closed completely on 2 September 1967, being demolished by March 1968. However, the station clock tower still remains and is part of the Victoria Shopping Centre, which was built on the site.

The famous railway town (now city) of Derby is our next location, as Class 3F 0–6–0 tank locomotive No. 47629 heads past the locomotive shed with a lightweight southbound freight on 16 June 1965. Note the 'Engine Sidings' signal-box of Midland Railway design. The locomotive depot closed to steam in March 1967. (*John Cooper-Smith*)

On Tuesday 17 May 1966, ex-LMS Class 8F No. 48067 heads north out of Chesterfield with a Derby–Sheffield mixed-goods train. On the right-hand side are sidings and a small scrapyard. Behind the photographer on the scrap line siding were a pair of ex-LNER Class B1 4–6–0s, Nos 61384 and 61223, awaiting their fate.

One of the wonderful anachronisms of the last days of BR steam was the Cromford & High Peak Railway (CHPR/LNWR), which survived with steam traction until its closure on Sunday 30 April 1967. This line, which opened in 1830, ran from High Peak Junction at Cromford (on the MR Derby–Manchester route) to Parsley Hay, where it connected with the former LNWR Ashbourne–Buxton line. The photograph above, taken on 20 May 1966 at the southern end of the line, shows ex-LMS Class 0F 0–4–0 saddle tank No. 47000 as it propels a load of wagons from Sheep Pasture to Middleton Quarry. Note the mixture of wagons. Below, a little later, No. 47000 is seen shunting at Middleton Quarry. The last day of the CHPR, 30 April 1967, saw several special brake van trains hauled between Middleton Top and Hopton by ex-LNER (WD) Class J94 0–6–0 saddle tanks Nos 68006 and 68012. With Middleton Quarry in the background, the 0–6–0STs are seen (opposite, top) climbing towards the 113-yard-long Hopton tunnel with a midday special to Hopton, and the photograph below (opposite, bottom) shows them returning to Middleton Top. These specials, which were organised by the Stephenson Locomotive Society (SLS), certainly attracted the crowds for the 'last rites' on the line – note the number of cars on the top right-hand side.

At the northern end of the Derby–Manchester line is Chinley Junction, where the line meets the Sheffield–Manchester route. Ex-LMS Class 8F 2–8–0 No. 48329 (off Heaton Mersey shed, 9F) makes a fine sight as it heads south out of Chinley for Peak Forest with an Up ballast train on 20 March 1967. This section of the line is still open to Peak Forest and sees a great deal of mineral traffic. Steam workings survived on this route until March 1968. (*John Cooper-Smith*)

Opposite, top: The MR main line from Derby to Manchester was closed between Matlock (some 6 miles north of Ambergate Junction, which was the junction for the Derby–Chesterfield route) and Peak Forest in 1968. Happily, however, a section of the line has been preserved from Matlock Riverside station to Rowsley South by the Peak Railway Society, and the line is known as the Peak Rail. It is also hoped one day to run through to Buxton. On 20 May 1966, when the line was fully open, we see a BR Standard Class 9F heading over Millers Dale viaduct with a southbound mineral train. There were four tracks at this location, carried on two adjacent viaducts. Millers Dale was also the junction station for the spa town of Buxton.

Opposite, bottom: Across in North Staffordshire, the Stoke on Trent area still had some steam activity in 1966. On the evening of Sunday 24 April 1966, a visit to Stoke shed (5D) saw a reasonable number of locomotives in steam, including ex-LMS 'Black Five' 4–6–0 No. 45060. Also on shed on that sunny evening were 9F 2–10–0s Nos 92101 and 92102, 2–6–0s Nos 43018 and 43112, as well as 'Black Fives' Nos 44968, 45191 and 45284, and 0–6–0 tank No. 47273.

Ex-LMS Class 8F 2–6–0 No. 48545 comes off the Birmingham line at Wigston North Junction with coal empties for the Leicester area, on 17 December 1965. The lines on the left are the MR route to St Pancras, and the centre line is to Rugby, this line closing in the late 1960s. (*John Cooper-Smith*)

We are still on the Leicester–Birmingham route, this time at Nuneaton, where, on 19 October 1965, ex-LMS Class 5MT 4–6–0 No. 45310 and 8F 2–8–0 No. 48111 double-head a Birmingham-bound goods train out of Nuneaton Abbey Street yard. (*John Cooper-Smith*)

We now move into Oxfordshire, where steam was still to be seen throughout most of 1966, not only on freight workings but also on the York–Bournemouth passenger trains, which were steam-worked between Banbury and Bournemouth. Oxford shed had closed by the end of 1965, but Banbury depot remained open until October 1966. The Bournemouth–York train is seen on the four-track section just north of Oxford at Wolvercote Junction (junction of the Banbury and Worcester lines) on 25 August 1966, hauled by Class 5MT No. 45493. An earlier photograph, taken on Saturday 13 August 1966, shows the southbound working as it heads over Aynho water troughs, just south of Banbury, hauled by BR Standard Class 5MT No. 73093. On the extreme left-hand side can be seen the spire of King's Sutton's fifteenth-century church. Note also the SR discs.

An immaculate-looking BR Class 9F 2–10–0 No. 92013 peers out of the gloom of Banbury shed on the morning of Saturday 26 February 1966. Behind the 9F is Class 5MT 4–6–0 No. 44865. No. 92013 was built in May 1954 and withdrawn from Saltley shed (2F) in September 1966 – a short life indeed! Banbury was originally a Western Region shed with the code 84C. However, this was changed to 2D when the area came under Midland Region control in the mid-1960s. (*Ken Blocksidge/Roger Siviter collection*)

Moving 9 miles north out of Banbury on the former GWR route to Birmingham Snow Hill we come to Fenny Compton, former junction station for the Stratford-upon-Avon & Midland Junction Railway (SMJR) route from Ravenstone Wood Junction, on the MR Northampton–Bedford line, to Stratford-upon-Avon and Broom Junction on the Redditch–Ashchurch line. This photograph, taken just south-east of Fenny Compton station on 18 September 1965, shows ex-GWR 'Manor' Class 4–6–0 No. 7821 (formerly *Ditcheat Manor*) on an Up fitted freight train. In the background can be clearly seen the SMJR line, which (apart from a small section from Fenny Compton to just east of Kineton for MoD traffic) had closed earlier that year. (*Michael Mensing*)

Tyseley shed (2A, formerly 84E) closed to steam in November 1966, and so in consequence steam workings could still be seen on the former GWR lines around Birmingham throughout most of that year. On 12 March 1966, Ivatt Class 2MT 2–6–0 No. 46470 looks worse for wear but is still going like a 'good un' as it nears the summit of Hatton bank, 1 in 110, with a neat-looking tank train. (*Michael Mensing*)

By 1966, with the exception of a few pannier tanks and 'Castle' Class No. 7029, GWR locomotives had more or less disappeared from the Birmingham area. However, in 1965 there were still a few examples left of the many classes of locomotives that were once to be seen there. Most of them were shorn of their attractive cabside plates (as well as name-plates). Fortunately, ex-GWR Class 2800 2–8–0 No. 3864 still retained its number-plate on 11 May 1965 as it was photographed, just south of Lapworth, with an Up empty iron-ore train bound for Banbury, probably emanating from the Black Country. These handsome 2–8–0 freight locomotives were originally designed by Churchward and introduced in 1903. No. 3864 was one of a number introduced in 1938 by Collett with design modifications. (*Michael Mensing*)

At around 8a.m. on Tuesday 1 June 1966, ex-LMS Class 8F 2–8–0 No. 48035 heads south on the four-track section near Bentley Heath with a Birmingham–Banbury goods. By now, with regional changes in the area, 8Fs, 2–8–0s and the 'Black Five' 4–6–0s had replaced the former GWR locomotives.

'Castle' Class No. 7029 *Clun Castle* speeds through the fog just north of Bentley Heath with the 'Talyllyn Railway Preservation Society' AGM special train on 24 September 1966. This train left Paddington at around 8a.m. and ran to Towyn (terminus of the Talyllyn Railway) via High Wycombe, Birmingham Snow Hill and Shrewsbury, the 'Castle' coming off at Shrewsbury, to be replaced by BR Standard Class 4MT 4–6–0s for the journey along the picturesque Cambrian route to Towyn.

The 17.35 Birmingham Snow Hill–Lapworth train arrives at Acocks Green & South Yardley station on 2 July 1965, hauled by BR Standard Class 5MT 4–6–0 No. 73013 off Wolverhampton Oxley shed (2B, formerly 84B). This working was one of the last handful of peak-period local trains on this route to remain steam worked (all with corridor stock) by this time. (*Michael Mensing*)

A few days later, on 17 July 1965, another member of the class, No. 73156, is seen leaving Bordesley with a Birmingham Snow Hill–Leamington stopping train. In the background is the LMR Camp Hill relief line, which runs from Landor Street Junction near Saltley on the Derby line to Kings Norton on the Birmingham–Bristol line. This is mainly a freight line, but it is also used as a Birmingham New Street avoiding line. (*John Cooper-Smith*)

Ex-GWR 'Grange' Class 4–6–0 No. 6853 (formerly *Morehampton Grange*) emerges from Snow Hill tunnel into Snow Hill station with a northbound freight on 17 July 1965. This fine old GWR station was closed to traffic in 1972 and demolished in 1977. I and many thousands of people still remember it with great affection. The sight of a Great Western 'King' Class locomotive on a Paddington express as you came down the stairs from the booking hall on to platform seven is something I will never forget. (*John Cooper-Smith*)

The 07.55 Birmingham–Aberystwyth train runs through Monmore Green, just south of Wolverhampton Low Level station, hauled by ex-GWR 'Manor' Class 4–6–0 No. 7829 *Ramsbury Manor*, on 24 July 1965. These 4–6–0s were designed by Collett, and introduced in 1938. No. 7829, the last of the class, being built in December 1950, was also the final one to be withdrawn, in December 1965. Happily, several examples remain in preservation. (*Ken Hale*)

The former GWR line between Wolverhampton Low Level and Shrewsbury saw steam action until the end of the through workings from Paddington on 5 March 1967. On 20 September 1965, ex-GWR 'Modified Hall' Class 4–6–0 No. 6964 *Thornbridge Hall* crosses Oxley viaduct, to the north-west of Wolverhampton, with the 17.20 Shrewsbury–Wolverhampton Low Level local train. This class of locomotive was introduced in 1944 and was a Hawksworth development of the Collett 'Hall' Class, which was introduced in 1928. No. 6964 was withdrawn from service shortly after this photograph was taken. (*Ken Hale*)

On the morning of Wednesday 20 November 1966, BR Standard Class 9F 2–10–0 No. 92084 climbs towards Codsall with a lightweight tank train from Shrewsbury to Wolverhampton, probably originating at Ellesmere Port. These sturdy freight locomotives were first introduced in 1954, No. 92084 being built in 1956 and withdrawn from Birkenhead shed (6C) in November 1967.

The line from Birmingham to Kidderminster, and on to Highley on the Severn Valley line, still saw a fair number of steam workings through to the autumn of 1966, when Tyseley shed closed to steam. One very interesting working which survived with steam throughout most of 1966 was the Halesowen branch, which ran from Old Hill on the Birmingham–Kidderminster line. It had originally run through from Halesowen to Longbridge on the Birmingham–Bristol line, but this section was closed in 1963. There was a regular afternoon goods train from Halesowen to Stourbridge which served Somers steel works, situated close by Halesowen station. There was also a connection from the goods yard up to the works' canal basin. The line had the distinction of, more often than not, being worked by some of the last GWR 0–6–0 pannier tank locomotives in service. This view, taken on 12 March 1966, shows Class 57XX pannier tank No. 8718 pausing during shunting duties by Halesowen signal-box.

Because of the steep climb from Halesowen up to Old Hill tunnel, and also the reversal at Old Hill station to gain the Stourbridge line, two locomotives were required. On 10 May 1966, 0–6–0 pannier tank Class 57XX No. 9614 banks the afternoon goods to Stourbridge out of Halesowen yard. The train is being hauled by another Class 57XX, No. 9608. In the background can be seen part of Somers steel works.

No. 4646 nears Old Hill tunnel and the summit of the climb from Halesowen with the Stourbridge goods train on Tuesday 16 August 1966. The banker is another member of the same class, No. 3607. Note also the wooden wagons. The Class 57XX 0–6–0 pannier tanks were introduced in 1929, and were designed by Collett for shunting and light goods work. No. 4646 was one of the last three surviving members of the class, being withdrawn (together with Nos 4696 and 9774) on 12 November 1966.

Below: On Sunday 11 September 1966, a special train organised by the Stephenson Locomotive Society was run around the Birmingham area, hauled by 0–6–0 pannier tanks of the Class 57XX Nos 9630 and 9610. This special charter, which included a trip down the Halesowen branch, was named 'Farewell to the GWR 0–6–0 PTs'. The train is seen leaving Old Hill tunnel (at the rear of the train) and heading down the bank to Halesowen. The special also travelled on to Dudley and Wolverhampton, and then back to Snow Hill for a trip down the North Warwick line to Stratford-upon-Avon – all for 21s!

This scene shows the banker, Class 2MT 2–6–0 No. 46470, on a Halesowen–Stourbridge goods passing the single line token, having just worked into Old Hill on 2 September 1966. The front locomotive is 0–6–0 PT No. 4696.

Ex-GWR 0–6–0PT No. 4646, having banked the Stourbridge goods out of Halesowen, gains the line to Stourbridge at Old Hill on 22 August 1966. The train locomotive from Halesowen, No. 3619, is now at the rear. I was lucky that I lived locally, and so was able to photograph this fascinating branch line throughout most of 1966, when steam was still in charge. The line closed completely in 1969.

Below: Stourbridge shed (2C, formerly 84F) on Sunday 13 March 1966. This was a typical GWR roundhouse depot, with twenty-eight roads off the central turntable. It had always been home to mainly freight and shunting locomotives, as well as a few passenger tank engines to work the local services to Birmingham Snow Hill and the Worcester area. By this time the shed came under the LM Region, and so, clustered round the turntable, there are three ex-LMS Class 8F 2–8–0s, Nos 48468, 48412 and 48121, as well as BR Standard Class 5MT 4–6–0 No. 73065. It was also still home to a few ex-GWR pannier tanks, used on local trip workings and shunting duties. The shed closed to steam on 11 July 1966, and completely by the end of that year.

An empty coal train, hauled by 8F 2–8–0 No. 48550, is photographed between Stourbridge Junction and Hagley as it hurries towards Kidderminster on Tuesday 5 July 1966. It is probably bound for Arley/Highley colliery on the Severn Valley line, where the coal trains to Stourport power station and further afield were still worked by steam until 11 July 1966, when the shed at Stourbridge closed to steam. This could well have been one of the last steam-worked coal trains in the area.

On the Thursday of the previous week (30 June 1966), 8F 2–8–0 No. 48531 heads through Bewdley station with a full load of coal for Stourport power station from Highley colliery. Bewdley is of course now part of the famous Severn Valley Railway preserved line from Kidderminster to Bridgnorth. It will no doubt be noticed by many people that happily very little change has occurred in the station area between 1966 and the present day.

Steam workings around the Worcester area finished with the closure of Worcester shed (85A) to steam at the end of 1965. On 15 May 1965, ex-GWR 'Grange' Class 4–6–0 No. 6841 (formerly *Marlas Grange*) approaches Norton Junction with the 14.23 train from Morton-in-Marsh to Worcester Shrub Hill. This Saturdays-only train, which originated at Oxford, was the last steam passenger working on the WR Oxford–Evesham–Worcester route, and would finish on 19 June 1965. In the foreground are the lines to Cheltenham and Gloucester. (*Michael Mensing*)

Class 9F 2–10–0 No. 92244 speeds along the four-track section at Churchdown, between Gloucester and Cheltenham, with a northbound steel train on 26 June 1965. (*Michael Mensing*)

These two photographs show the Birmingham–Stratford-upon-Avon–Cheltenham route in 1965, the last summer of steam workings on the line. The first scene shows 'Grange' Class 4–6–0 No. 6827 (formerly *Llanfrechfa Grange*) with the 12.30 Penzance–Wolverhampton Low Level as it approaches Hunting Butts tunnel, just north of Cheltenham Spa, on 26 June 1965. The GWR 'Grange' Class was designed by Collett and introduced in 1936. It is said that the 'Granges', together with Churchward's elegant Class 47XX 2–8–0s, were the finest engines ever built by the Great Western Railway. Sadly, no examples of either class survive into preservation. The second photograph was taken at the northern end of this route, just south of Henley-in-Arden, on what is known as the North Warwicks line, between Stratford-upon-Avon and Birmingham Snow Hill. On 21 August 1965, Standard Class 5MT 4–6–0 No. 73014 approaches Henley-in-Arden with the 11.10 Ilfracombe–Wolverhampton Low Level service. By this time, the service was usually diesel-hauled, so No. 73014 is obviously deputising for a failed diesel locomotive. (*Both: Michael Mensing*)

Chapter Four
Yorkshire & the North-East

Copy Pit summit on the Burnley to Todmorden line is 749ft above sea level, and roughly on the Lancashire–Yorkshire border. This was mainly a freight line, with many of the heavier trains requiring banking assistance. Northbound the gradient is 1 in 65, and southbound from Burnley 1 in 68. On 8 October 1966, ex-LMS Class 8F 2–8–0 No. 48435 heads south past Copy Pit signal-box, having just banked a heavy northbound freight up to the summit. After returning to Hall Royd Junction at Todmorden, it will then await its next banking duty. Steam on this line lasted until the very end, Rose Grove shed (10F) at Burnley being one of the very last sheds to close, at the end of July 1968 (see Chapter Six).

Also on Saturday 8 October 1966, the north-west branch of the Locomotive Club of Great Britain (LCGB) ran a 'Hughes Crab' commemorative tour from Liverpool to Manchester, Accrington, Todmorden, Halifax, Wakefield and Goole, and back via the Calder Valley route and Manchester to Liverpool. The special charter is seen on the outward journey in somewhat murky conditions at Copy Pit summit, with 'Black Five' 4–6–0 No. 45346 and Crab 2–6–0 No. 42942 in charge. Note the two photographers on the left-hand side!

We are now at Keighley in the West Riding, where, on 23 June 1966, ex-LMS 'Jubilee' Class 4–6–0 No. 45675 *Hardy* takes water before leaving with a Down parcels train. This is probably the 09.15 Leeds–Carlisle parcels, which at the time was steam-worked, often by a 'Jubilee' locomotive off Leeds Holbeck shed (55A). (*B.J. Ashworth*)

An evening spent at Skipton on 11 July 1966 shows, first of all, at around 8.45p.m., ex-LMS Fairburn Class 4MT 2–6–4 tank No. 42105 shunting. These locomotives were first introduced in 1945, and were a development of an earlier Stanier design. In the background can be seen Class 2MT 2–6–2 tank No. 41241. A few minutes later, and the 20.01 service from Leeds to Skipton approaches the station with 4–6–0 No. 44852 in charge. Note the Midland signal-box.

On 13 September 1966, BR Standard Class 9F 2–10–0 No. 92093 climbs up to Ais Gill summit (1,169ft above sea level) with a southbound mineral train. Steam was still active on this scenic Pennine route until the end of 1967, although by this time the traffic was sparse. I spent most of the day on the line and, according to my records, saw six steam workings. I suppose that is why most people photographed on the WCML around Tebay and Shap, where at the time you could probably see around four to six steam workings in an hour!

Opposite, top: Another view of the 09.15 Leeds–Carlisle parcels train, this time approaching Dent station on the MR Settle–Carlisle route. Once again, it is hauled by 'Jubilee' Class 4–6–0 No. 45675 *Hardy*, and the date is 15 September 1966. Although the engine looks in poor external condition, it was still running very well. Note the snow fences – very important at this location, as Dent station, at around 1,000ft above sea level, is the highest in England.

Opposite, bottom: The summer of 1966 was obviously a busy time for one of the last remaining LMS 'Jubilee' Class 4–6–0s, No. 45675 *Hardy*. Here it is once again, this time in the early hours of Saturday 23 July 1966, waiting to leave Sheffield Midland station with the 02.00 train to Leeds. It is also a reminder that at one time (certainly from city stations) it was possible to catch a train throughout the night. I personally remember making many non-sleeper night journeys, especially in the 1950s. (*Ken Hale*)

A beautiful photograph of another member of the 6P5F 'Jubilee' Class, this time No. 45647 *Sturdee* hauling the 08.19 Leeds–Bradford parcels train near Calverley & Rodley station on 18 March 1967. Note the shed code – 55A (Leeds Holbeck). (*Ken Hale*)

On Tuesday 12 July 1966, our old friend No. 45675 *Hardy* waits to leave Leeds City station with the 20.43 train to Sheffield Midland. The last of the 191 members of this famous class were withdrawn by the autumn of 1967, and several examples are preserved, but sadly not No. 45675.

Happily, one member of the 'Jubilee' Class that was preserved (at Tyseley Railway Museum) was No. 45593 *Kholapur*, seen here inside Leeds Holbeck shed on 13 February 1967. Over the years since preservation, it has made many fine runs on special charter trains, including several trips on the S&C route between Leeds and Carlisle. The LMS 'Jubilee' Class was first introduced in 1934, and designed by Sir William A. Stanier, FRS. (*John Cooper-Smith*)

Bradford Manningham shed (55F) plays host to ex-LMS Fairburn Class 4MT 2–6–4 tanks Nos 42189 and 42152 on 18 February 1967. At the time, these locomotives were used not only for shunting and freight duties, but often on the Bradford–Wakefield three- or four-coach portion of the Leeds–Kings Cross trains, the main train being hauled by an English Electric Deltic locomotive. (*John Cooper-Smith*)

On 30 September 1967, the 09.55 Bradford–Wakefield portion of the Leeds–Kings Cross Pullman service pulls out of Bradford Exchange station, this time hauled, not by a 2–6–4 tank, but by ex-LNER Class B1 4–6–0 No. 61306. These attractive 4–6–0s were first introduced on the LNER in 1942, and were designed by Thompson. (*Ken Hale*)

By the end of 1967, steam had more or less finished in the Yorkshire area. However, during the previous year, especially round the Wakefield area, there still seemed to be almost an abundance of steam turns, notably with coal and general freight traffic. A visit of around three hours to Wakefield Kirkgate station on the morning of Thursday 22 September 1966 saw about a dozen steam turns with a variety of locomotives, including a 'Britannia' Pacific, 'Jubilee' 4–6–0, B1 4–6–0, 'Black Five' 4–6–0, Fairburn 2–6–4 tank and several ex-WD Class 8F 2–8–0s, including No. 90617, seen here waiting to leave Kirkgate station with a westbound coal train. The mixed freight passing by was also hauled by a WD 2–8–0, No. 90417.

Above and opposite: Of the many lines around the Wakefield area, one of the busiest for steam-worked freight trains in 1966 was that from Goole, the dockland town on the River Humber in the East Riding of Yorkshire. On a sunny Monday 19 September 1966, ex-WD 8F 2–8–0 No. 90132 approaches the outskirts of Wakefield with a heavy coal train from the Goole direction. The bridge in the extreme background carries the Midland line from Normanton to Cudworth. Turning round from the previous view, we see another WD 2–8–0, No. 90091, as it heads for Wakefield on the following day (20 September) with another load of coal from the Goole area. We complete this trio of coal trains with BR Standard Class 9F 2–10–0 No. 92090 heading east out of Wakefield on the line to Goole on Wednesday 13 July 1966.

On 18 February 1967, WD 8F 2–8–0 No. 90450 was photographed at Hull Dairycoates shed (50B). These rugged Ministry of Supply 'Austerity' locomotives were first introduced in 1943, and designed by Riddles. They were purchased by British Railways in 1948, and remained in service until the end of 1967. (*John Cooper-Smith*)

The impressive-looking station of Church Fenton, some 11 miles south of York on the York–Leeds route, is the next location, as ex-LNER Class B1 4–6–0 No. 61337 hurries through with a northbound goods on the morning of Thursday 26 May 1966. Church Fenton is also the junction for the York–Sheffield line. Note the very ornate station lamps and station chimney pots, and also the locomotive shed code – 50A York.

On 21 September 1966, ex-LNER Class K1 2–6–0 No. 62012 is seen just north of Church Fenton near Colton with the midday freight for York from the Leeds area. These 2–6–0s were introduced on the Eastern Region just after nationalisation in 1949.

We are still on the route from York to Leeds, this time near Copmanthorpe, some 4 miles south of the ancient Roman city, and the train is a York–Leeds mixed freight, hauled by ex-LMS 'Jubilee' Class 4–6–0 No. 45593 *Kholapur* on 21 September 1966. The locomotive looks in nice external condition, and is complete with a yellow stripe on the cabside, denoting that the engine must avoid working under electric catenary. Note also how lovely and trim is the 'Permanent Way'.

Another K1 Class 2–6–0, No. 62028, propels empty coaching stock into the north end of York station on 26 May 1966. This ECS train then formed the 09.35 service to Kings Cross – to be operated by diesel traction. Although these powerful 2–6–0s (they had a tractive effort of 32,080lb) were built for passenger or freight use (5P6F), by 1966 they were often to be found on shunting and station pilot duties. No. 62028 was withdrawn from service in December 1966. Worthy of note are the elegant diamond crossovers.

Steam in the North-East around the Hartlepool, Sunderland and Newcastle area lasted until September 1967. One of the most fascinating aspects of the steam turns was the use of pre-Grouping locomotives from the North Eastern Railway (NER). In particular, two classes remained until the end of steam, Class Q6 0–8–0 and Class J27 0–6–0, the 0–8–0s having been introduced in 1913 and the 0–6–0s in 1906. Class Q6 No. 63450 climbs a steep grade near Monk Heseldene with the 09.00 West Hartlepool to Shotton Colliery on 22 October 1966. (*Ken Hale*)

On 23 June 1966, Class J27 No. 65814 climbs between Scots Gap and Woodburn with the Thursdays-only 10.25 Morpeth to Woodburn goods. This train was run to service the TA camp at Woodburn. The line from Morpeth on the ECML was originally North British, and ran to Riccarton Junction on the Waverley route via Reedsmouth.

The final photographs in this section show the last steam-worked passenger line in the North-East, from Alnmouth (on the ECML) to Alnwick in Northumberland. Class K1 2–6–0s were the usual locomotives for this short branch. However, on 1 June 1966, ex-LNER Class V2 2–6–2 No. 60836 worked the line. The first view shows the powerful 2–6–2 arriving at Alnwick past the NER signal-box with the 16.48 from Alnmouth, and the second scene shows No. 60836 inside the impressive NER terminus station at Alnwick, waiting to leave with the two-coach 17.55 train to Alnmouth. A far cry from crack express and freight workings on the ECML! This branch line became diesel-operated on 18 June 1966, and closed altogether on 29 January 1968. (*Both: Hugh Ballantyne*)

Chapter Five
Scotland

We start our Scottish journey in Ayrshire, where in 1966 there was still an allocation of locomotives at Ayr shed (67C), principally for working the branch lines that served the Ayrshire coalfield. At Annbank Junction on 24 June 1966, Class 5 4–6–0 No. 45167 with a train of empty coal wagons takes the branch line to Drongan and Killoch, while 4–6–0 No. 44989 waits to come off the Mauchline–Auchinleck line with a mixed freight for Ayr. Steam more or less finished in Ayrshire in December 1966, with the closure of Ayr shed.

'Jubilee' 4–6–0 No. 45647 *Sturdee* (shedded at Leeds Holbeck) hurries through Barrhead in the outer suburbs of Glasgow with the 16.05 Glasgow–Leeds relief train on Good Friday, 24 March 1967. This locomotive had been thoroughly cleaned by the 'Neverers' and may well have been the last working by a 'Jubilee' in Scotland. One thing is worth recounting: this train originally should have been eight coaches, but when the 'lads' were at Corkerhill shed (67A) in Glasgow, they were told that the load was to be nine coaches, so necessitating a Type 2 diesel on the front of the train. But as the name implies, the 'Neverers' never gave up, and they persuaded the shed foreman to let the 4–6–0 take the nine-coach load on its own – and so we have this magnificent picture. (*Ken Hale*)

The West Coast Main Line (WCML) between Carlisle and Glasgow still had steam workings through to May 1967, when steam finished in Scotland. A popular area of the WCML to photograph was Beattock bank – 10 miles of around 1 in 75. Banking assistance was provided by the small shed at Beattock (66F), usually by ex-LMS Class 4MT 2–6–4 tank engines, and also by BR Standard Class 4MT 2–6–0 tender locomotives. On 24 June 1966, Fairburn 2–6–4 tank No. 42058 banks a heavy tank train out of Beattock station. On the extreme right-hand side is the locomotive depot, and on the left-hand side a pair of breakdown cranes.

Working hard on Beattock bank is Class 5MT No. 45176, climbing through the cutting north of Greskine box with a Down mineral train on 31 May 1966. The train is banked by Stanier 2–6–4 tank No. 42694. Greskine signal-box is situated roughly halfway on the 10-mile climb. (*Hugh Ballantyne*)

The famous 'Waverley Route' (which closed in 1969), from Carlisle to Edinburgh via Riccarton Junction and Galashiels, saw regular steam freight and some steam passenger workings until the end of 1965. Class V2 2–6–2 No. 60835 works hard just south of Whitrope with the 08.35 Edinburgh Millerhill–Carlisle Kingmoor goods on 21 August 1965. *Opposite, top:* On 30 October 1965, Class B1 4–6–0 No. 61345 was photographed near Whitrope with the 11.15 Kingmoor–Millerhill freight. Whitrope is situated just south of Riccarton Junction. *Opposite, bottom:* A 'Waverley Route' passenger train leaving Edinburgh on 17 July 1965. The train is the 09.50 from Edinburgh to Leeds (via both the Waverley and the S&C routes), hauled by the last of the ex-LMS 'Royal Scot' Class 4–6–0s in service, No. 46115 *Scots Guardsman*. Happily, this locomotive has been preserved. The location is Calton tunnel, just south of Waverley station. Note the locomotive shed code, 12A Carlisle Kingmoor. (*All: Ken Hale*)

Scotland was the final home for the last of the ex-LNER Pacific locomotives. Classes A2, A3 and particularly Sir Nigel Gresley's Class A4 locomotives were to be found at work in the last years of steam north of the border. The Class A4s were the regular engines for the Glasgow–Aberdeen trains, which they worked until September 1966. However, during that period they would occasionally work between Edinburgh and Aberdeen, as on 16 July 1966, when A4 Pacific No. 60034 *Lord Faringdon* is seen leaving The Mound tunnel as it heads out of Waverley station with the 10.30 to Aberdeen. The station can be seen through the right-hand tunnel portal. Above the tunnel is the National Gallery. (*Ken Hale*)

The most powerful ex-LNER Pacific locomotives were the Class A2s. These were introduced in 1947 and were a Peppercorn development of an earlier Thompson design. In 1966, their last active year, three members of the class were still to be found in Scotland – Nos 60528 *Tudor Minstrel*, 60530 *Sayajirao* and 60532 *Blue Peter* – but only No. 60532 was to be seen on regular passenger train workings, notably the 13.30 Aberdeen–Glasgow service. *Blue Peter* is seen in a sylvan setting near Cumbernauld with the 13.30 Aberdeen–Glasgow train on 16 July 1966. This locomotive has been preserved and has seen much work on main-line charter trains. (*Ken Hale*)

This view of the Forth Bridge was taken from North Queensferry on 17 July 1965, and shows one of the last of the ex-LNER Gresley A3 Class Pacifics in action – No. 60052 *Prince Palatine*. The train is the 14.25 Edinburgh Waverley to Dundee. This class, which includes probably the most famous steam locomotive in the world, *Flying Scotsman*, was introduced in 1927, and by 1966 they had all been withdrawn, the only survivor into preservation being, of course, *Flying Scotsman*. (*Ken Hale*)

The 13.30 Aberdeen–Glasgow train once again, hauled by No. 60532 on 25 June 1966. The location is Auchterarder viaduct, 2 miles north of Gleneagles in Perthshire. (*Ken Hale*)

Several examples of the ex-LNER B1 4–6–0s were to be found in Scotland right up to the end of steam in the spring of 1967. On 20 June 1966, B1 No. 61349 runs round its goods train at Bridge of Earn before leaving for Perth. This location is on the Ladybank route through Fife to Edinburgh. Bridge of Earn was also the junction for the 'Glenfarg' route to the capital via Cowdenbeath, which closed in 1965.

Former LNER Class B1 4–6–0 No. 61330 pulls out of Perth on the morning of Saturday 18 June 1966 with a southbound train of empty coal wagons, and runs past sidings full of coaching stock and parcels vans. Overlooking the scene is the Dewar whisky distillery. Note also the abundance of chimney pots and the variety of telegraph poles.

Class J38 0–6–0 No. 65921 runs through North Queensferry station and approaches the northern end of the Forth Bridge with the 15.20 Alloa–Edinburgh Millerhill freight on 17 July 1965. No. 65921 was one of many members of this sturdy class of goods engine to be shedded at Thornton shed (62A). (*Ken Hale*)

Opposite, top: During Scotland's final summer of steam workings (1966), one of the many interesting steam turns was the 08.29 empty coaching stock (ECS) train from Dundee to Perth. This would, more often than not, produce one of Dundee shed's (62B) famous but ever-diminishing fleet of ex-LNER Gresley Class V2 2–6–2 locomotives. On this occasion, 21 June 1966, No. 60813 is seen in charge of the ECS train as it crosses over Tay Street just before entering Perth station. No. 60813 was fitted with mini smoke deflectors. The adverts are worthy of note – no health warnings in those days!

Opposite, bottom: On a very cold Tuesday 28 March 1967, ex-LNER Class B1 4–6–0 No. 61102 nears Maryfield (just north of Dundee) with a Dundee–Maryfield coal train. This former Caledonian Railway branch line (now closed), together with the line to Alyth Junction, came off the Dundee–Perth line at Ninewells Junction, just to the west of Dundee station. (*Ken Hale*)

The following summer (21 June 1966) sees sister engine No. 65914 climbing wrong-line working out of Thornton Junction with a heavy coal train bound for Dunfermline. The location is Cluny, a mile or so west of Thornton. These Class 6F 0–6–0s were designed by Sir Nigel Gresley and introduced on the LNER in 1936. Primarily intended for heavy freight work, they would occasionally appear on passenger workings. Of the thirty-five members of the class, sadly none survived into preservation. No. 65914 was withdrawn in November 1966.

An hour or so before the previous photograph was taken, and at the same location, we see another Class J38 0–6–0, this time No. 65929, heading for Thornton Junction with a mixed-freight train from the Dunfermline area. No. 65929 was one of the last members of the class in service, being withdrawn in April 1967. Note the difference in the signal poles, the modern BR pole on the right contrasting with the North British pole on the left-hand side of the track.

At one time, Thornton shed (62A) was home to ninety-four locomotives, including several pre-Grouping 0–6–0 tender engines. One example which survived through to 1966, albeit stored in the shed yard, was Class J36 0–6–0 No. 65327, seen here at Thornton on a sunny Thursday 16 June 1966. These locomotives were designed by Holmes for the North British Railway, and introduced in 1888. At the rear of No. 65327 is an unidentified Class J38 0–6–0.

We leave the kingdom of Fife and the former coal-mining area around Thornton Junction, and head north for Angus and Brechin city. The Brechin branch, which ran from Bridge of Dun on the Kinnaber to Stanley Junction (for Perth) Caledonian line, saw a daily steam-worked freight from Montrose until 7 April 1967. The motive power for the branch train was provided by a former North British Class J37 0–6–0 locomotive, shedded at Montrose. On 15 June 1966, No. 64547 is seen shunting at Brechin, and a little later, about a mile east of Brechin, en route to Bridge of Dun and Montrose with the afternoon goods train. The Brechin branch closed in 1981, but happily the branch has been preserved and is known as the Caledonian Railway (Brechin). The Caledonian route between Kinnaber Junction and Stanley Junction closed completely by June 1982.

On a wet midsummer day in 1966 (15 June), A4 Pacific No. 60034 *Lord Faringdon* hurries through the gloom near Kinnaber Junction with the 13.30 Aberdeen–Glasgow train – 'The Grampian'. Kinnaber Junction is the famous location from the 1890s, when East (North British) and West (Caledonian) Coast trains raced each other to the junction to be first into Aberdeen.

A few minutes before the previous photograph was taken, we see 'Black Five' 4–6–0 No. 44797 near Kinnaber Junction with the 12.25 Perth–Aberdeen parcels train. These 'maid of all work' locomotives were first introduced on the LMS in 1934, and designed by Stanier. They were to be found all over the system. They also had the distinction of hauling the very last BR steam train on 11 August 1968.

On 14 June 1966, A4 Pacific No. 60019 *Bittern* skirts the North Sea at Niggs Bay, just south of Aberdeen, with the 17.15 Aberdeen–Glasgow three-hour train. No. 60019 was one of several examples of this famous class not to be fitted with a corridor tender.

The final photograph in this section was taken at Aberdeen, the most northerly point in the UK from which steam was still operating by this time. On 14 June 1966, No. 60034 *Lord Faringdon* pulls out of Aberdeen Union Street station with the 13.30 train to Glasgow Buchanan Street. Unlike the other Aberdeen–Glasgow trains which were hauled by steam, the 13.30 service was allowed four hours for the run to Glasgow, but this included extra stops. Steam working on these trains finished in the following September, the last train being on 14 September, when A4 No. 60024 *Kingfisher* worked the 08.25 Glasgow to Aberdeen service. Note the busy-looking station goods yard on the right-hand side.

Chapter Six
The North-West

For obvious reasons, the final section is devoted to the North-West of England, where the last rites of BR steam were performed on 11 August 1968. The famous railway town of Crewe is our first location, where, on the night of 24 June 1966, ex-LMS Class 3F 0–6–0 tank No. 47530 pauses during shunting duties. Note the shed code, 5B Crewe South. (*Ken Hale*)

By April 1968, BR Standard Class 9F 2–10–0s were being withdrawn rapidly, but one of the main areas where they could still be seen at work was on the Cheshire Lines Committee (CLC) route between Widnes and Stockport. 9F 2–10–0 No. 92069, with a load of empty coal wagons from the Widnes area, hurries towards Stockport on 25 April 1968. The location is just east of Skelton Junction on the former CLC route. No. 92069 was built at Doncaster in December 1955, and was one of the last survivors of the class, being withdrawn in May 1968. Several examples remain in preservation, including the last locomotive built by BR, No. 92220 *Evening Star*.

Opposite: Crewe North shed (5A) had been the principal shed in the area with, at one time, 125 engines on its books, including LMS 'Coronation' and 'Princess' Class 4–6–2s, and also 'Royal Scot', 'Patriot' and 'Jubilee' 4–6–0s, but this shed had closed in 1965, leaving Crewe South, which was home to mainly goods locomotives, as the principal steam shed until it closed in 1967. On the evening of Sunday 24 April 1966, immaculate Class 9F 2–10–0 No. 92002 poses at the side of Crewe South shed, while at the front of the depot BR 'Britannia' Pacific No. 70012 (formerly *John of Gaunt*) is seen beside BR Standard Class 4MT 2–6–0 No. 76040 and 9F 2–10–0 No. 92032.

Above and opposite: The Stockport area in the north-east of Cheshire saw steam workings until the beginning of June 1968. The last two steam sheds in this area were Stockport Edgeley (9B) and Heaton Mersey (9F). This silhouette shot was taken at Stockport Edgeley shed on the late evening of 25 April 1968. On the left is the tender of Class 8F 2–8–0 No. 48267, and on the right-hand side is the front of 'Black Five' 4–6–0 No. 44868. Earlier that same evening, 8F No. 48720 was photographed at Heaton Mersey shed.

On Whit Saturday, 28 May 1966, ex-LMS Class 5MT 4–6–0 No. 44838 on a Down express takes water on Moore troughs, some 2 miles south of Warrington on the West Coast Main Line (WCML). The coaching stock was in the then-new blue and grey livery. (*Hugh Ballantyne*)

Above: Right until the end of steam, the former L&Y Victoria station at Manchester was always worth a visit. Class 4MT 2–6–4 tank No. 42656 is busy shunting a van train at the eastern end of the station on 17 June 1966. *Left*: Just under two years later, on 1 June 1968, and at the same location, 'Britannia' Pacific No. 70013 *Oliver Cromwell* departs with a return special charter to Edinburgh – the BR Scottish Region 'Grand Rail Tour No. 5'. By now, No. 70013 was the last member of the class in service, all the others having been withdrawn by the end of 1967.

Manchester Victoria station on 9 March 1968 sees 'Black Five' 4–6–0 No. 44890 shunting a van train in one of the outer platforms, probably No. 17.

This picture at Manchester Victoria station was taken on 1 June 1968, and shows the 'Miles Platting Bankers' on the station through roads. The locomotives are Class 8F 2–8–0 No. 48168 and Class 5MT 4–6–0 No. 45208. The through roads also connected Victoria with Manchester Exchange station. In the space of a couple of hours, I had seen around a dozen steam locomotives at this location, including 8Fs, 'Black Fives' and, of course, No. 70013 – and all this within a few weeks of the end of steam. Note the photographers on this glorious 1 June, all out to catch forever on film the dying embers of steam.

A final view of the outer platforms at Victoria station, again on 1 June 1968. In the foreground is 4–6–0 No. 45203 (on a van train), and in the background is sister engine No. 45420 in charge of another van/parcels train, which is being loaded.

I mentioned earlier that Victoria was connected to Exchange station (by the longest platform in the UK), and, like Victoria station, steam could still be seen in Exchange station in 1968, although mainly on shunting duties. On 9 March 1968, BR Standard Class 5MT 4–6–0 No. 73157 pauses during shunting duties in the former LNWR station. This station closed in 1969, the traffic being re-routed into Victoria. No. 73157 was built in December 1956, and was one of a number fitted with Caprotti valve gear. It was withdrawn from service in May 1968.

Another Manchester station that saw some activity in the latter days of steam was the former CLC Central station. On 31 March 1967, Class 5MT 4–6–0 No. 44895 arrives at the terminus station with an ECS train. This attractive station with its beautiful roof was opened by the CLC in 1880, and closed in 1969 when, for a time, it became a car park (it is a listed building). Finally, in 1986, it became an exhibition hall, and is known as the G-Mex Centre. (*John Cooper-Smith*)

Patricroft (9H) and Newton Heath (9D) locomotive sheds were the last steam sheds in Manchester, both closing at the end of June 1968. On 18 November 1967, BR Standard Class 5MT 4–6–0s No. 73053 and No. 73128 (fitted with Caprotti valve gear) receive attention at Patricroft shed. In its heyday, this shed was home to around eighty locomotives, including several 'Jubilee' Class 4–6–0s.

Bolton shed (9K), like Patricroft and Newton Heath, also closed at the end of June 1968. A visit to the shed on 6 June 1968 showed that there was still some steam activity in the area, with ex-LMS Class 5MT 4–6–0 No. 45318 awaiting its next duty. It is flanked by 8F 2–8–0s, with No. 48392 on the right-hand side and No. 48773 on the left. Also on shed that day were 'Black Fives' Nos 44947, 45073 and 45290. A further visit, on 19 July 1968, shows the shed now closed and with just one 'dead' locomotive on view, 4–6–0 No. 44947. Note the L&YR public notice on the right-hand side, a reminder of the shed's ancestry.

We leave the Manchester area and return to the WCML just south of Preston at Farrington East Junction, where, on 26 February 1968, Class 5MT 4–6–0 No. 45353 heads north with a mixed-goods train. The busy goods yard is a reminder of the days when the railways were the main freight carriers. The junction to Lostock Hall and the Blackburn line is just to the right of the signal-box. Also on the right-hand side can be seen the coaling tower at Lostock Hall MPD. The rail bridge in the background carries the Blackburn line to the Liverpool area, thus avoiding Preston station.

On the same day as the previous shot, Class 8F 2–8–0 No. 48393 heads through Lostock Hall Junction with an eastbound freight train from the Blackburn direction. On the left-hand side is the connecting line to the main Preston (station) to Blackburn line.

Lostock Hall shed (10D) at Preston had the distinction of supplying the locomotives for the final BR timetabled steam working on 3 August 1968, and also for the six special steam charter trains that were run on the following day. This was the scene at Lostock Hall shed on Sunday afternoon, 25 February 1968, as Class 5MT 4–6–0 No. 45345 is being prepared to work the 17.52 Preston–Liverpool service, one of the last regular steam passenger workings left on BR by this time (see also page 4). On the right-hand side is 8F 2–8–0 No. 48253, complete with shed code.

The views above and top right were both taken at around mid-morning on Monday 26 February 1968 from the southern end of Preston station, and show something of the wonderful variety of signalling that there was here, prior to the electrification of this area. An Up coal train, hauled by Class 5MT 4–6–0 No. 44761, is framed by one of the older gantries. On the left is the signal-box which controlled this immediate area, and in the distance can be seen more bracket and gantry signals. A Class 08 diesel shunter with a short van train completes the scene. The second picture, taken a few minutes earlier, shows another 'Black Five' 4–6–0, No. 44816, with a northbound freight train, passing under a more 'modern' gantry. These photographs were taken less than six months before the end of steam, but conceivably could have been taken in the late 1950s.

An earlier view, taken at Preston station on a very wet Friday 18 August 1967, shows the front end of 'Black Five' 4–6–0 No. 44709, which was waiting to leave on an Up parcels train. Prominent is Preston No. 2A signal-box, of LNWR design.

Above and opposite: These two views were again taken at Preston on 26 February 1968, only this time under the roof of the former LNWR station. In the scene above, taken at 11.35a.m., 4–6–0 No. 45134 is about to leave with a parcels train for the Carnforth area, while, 42 minutes later, sister engine No. 44890 departs with the 12.17 to Manchester Victoria, one of the last scheduled steam passenger workings in the timetable. In the foreground are the lines to Blackburn; note also the station signal-box.

This picture at Low Barn (near Houghton) was taken a few weeks later on 6 June 1968, and shows an immaculate-looking BR Standard Class 4MT 4–6–0 No. 75019 heading for Preston with a ballast train from Swinden quarry, situated on the Grassington branch, just north of Skipton. From these three pictures, it is very hard to imagine that the end of steam on British Railways was only a few weeks away.

Opposite: One of the busiest lines for steam workings, right up to the end of steam, was the Preston, Blackburn and Burnley route, the motive power generally being provided by Lostock Hall shed at Preston and Rose Grove shed at Burnley, both of which, together with Carnforth, were the final steam depots on the BR system. These two photographs were taken on this route at Low Barn near Houghton on 18 April 1968, and show first of all 'Black Five' 4–6–0 No. 45345 heading downgrade towards Preston with a coal train from the Burnley area. The second view shows Class 8F 2–8–0 No. 48423 climbing towards Blackburn with a train of empty coal wagons from the Preston direction. Considering the date, both locomotives are in very good external condition and, if my memory serves me right, also sounded in fine working order.

On the day that England won the World Cup, Saturday 30 July 1966, I spent most of the day on the Preston–Blackpool line around Lea water troughs, just to the east of Salwick station. They were one of only four sets of water troughs still on the BR system, and the only one with four tracks (although by 1968 these had been reduced to two tracks). This photograph shows a morning Stoke–Blackpool train, hauled by an unidentified 'Black Five' 4–6–0 off Stoke shed (5D).

A few minutes later the sun came out, and 4–6–0 No. 45259 (off Carlisle Kingmoor shed – 12A) came along with a Blackpool–Glasgow train.

The next train I photographed was a North Wales–Blackpool train, hauled by Class 5MT 4–6–0 No. 44661, which was shedded at Llandudno Junction (6G).

We complete the quartet with the 09.10 Dundee–Blackpool train, hauled by 'Britannia' Pacific No. 70018 *Flying Dutchman*. This 4–6–2, which was built in June 1951 and withdrawn in December 1966, was one of only two 'Britannias' that I saw on the Blackpool line that day, the other being No. 70006 *Robert Burns*.

After leaving the Blackpool line in the late afternoon, I stopped at Hazelmere on the WCML, just north of Preston, and was rewarded with a shot of 'Britannia' Pacific No. 70024 *Vulcan* on a Down evening passenger train.

Still on the West Coast Main Line, this time at Bailrigg, just south of Lancaster, where, on 18 April 1968, a very grimy 'Black Five' 4–6–0 No. 45095 heads north with a ballast train. Within a short time, this stretch of the WCML would be electrified and resignalled.

Above and opposite, bottom: The Carnforth–Skipton line saw steam workings right through to almost the end of BR steam, mainly to serve Swinden quarry on the Grassington branch (see also page 119). BR Standard Class 4 4–6–0 No. 75019, in very nice external condition, heads downgrade near Bentham with a train of empty wagons bound for Swinden quarry on 17 April 1968. Immediately after this photograph was taken, the train must have been held somewhere, for I was able to get by car to Clapham (only a few miles away) and secure the second shot of it crossing Clapham viaduct. Note also that by now the train is wrong-line working. Clapham was the junction station for Sedbergh and on to connect with the WCML at Low Gill, but this line closed in 1965.

This view of Carnforth shed (10A) was taken on Monday 27 June 1966, and gives a good idea of the locomotives still shedded there, including 'Britannia' Pacifics, BR Standard Class 9F 2–10–0s, 'Black Five' 4–6–0s and ex-LMS Class 4MT 2–6–0s. The shed closed in 1968 but was preserved, and is now known as Steamtown Railway Museum, with its own fleet of steam locomotives. (*B.J. Ashworth*)

As well as being on the WCML, and the junction station for the line to Hellifield and Skipton (for Leeds), Carnforth is also the junction for the old Furness Railway Cumbrian coast line to Barrow, Workington and on to Carlisle. On 18 June 1966, 'Britannia' Pacific No. 70020 *Mercury* approaches Silverdale station (just south of Arnside) with an Up express train, probably a Barrow–Euston service. (*B.J. Ashworth*)

The lengthy viaduct at Arnside, which crosses the River Kent where it runs into Morecambe Bay, is the setting as Class 5MT 4–6–0 No. 44709 runs off the viaduct and heads south towards Carnforth with a mixed-freight train on 17 April 1968. Steam survived in this area almost to the very end.

In 1967, the Whitehaven, Cleator and Egremont Joint (Furness and LNWR) line from Sellafield to Workington was still open, and in Egremont yard on Sunday 28 August 1967 ex-LMS Class 4MT 2–6–0 No. 43023 is seen on shunting duties. The coach on the left-hand side is worthy of note. This line closed completely in 1980.

A busy scene at Carnforth station on Saturday 18 June 1966. A northbound WCML parcels train is being loaded as the water in the tender of BR 'Britannia' Pacific No. 70011 *Hotspur* is replenished in readiness for the climb over the Cumbrian Fells to the Roman city of Carlisle. There is much to enjoy in this vintage scene. (*B.J. Ashworth*)

Some 13 miles north of Carnforth on the WCML is Oxenholme, junction station for the branch line to the famous resort of Windermere, set among the splendours of the Lake District. On a rather dull day, 30 August 1967, 'Britannia' Pacific No. 70024 *Vulcan* hurries down Grayrigg bank and enters Oxenholme station with a heavy southbound mixed-goods train. To the left of the train can be seen the branch line to Windermere. Note the ornate station lamp, next to the water column.

Throughout the summer of 1967, several passenger trains were still steam-hauled on the Windermere branch, including the 17.45 Windermere–Blackpool train, seen here departing from Windermere in fine style, hauled by 'Black Five' 4–6–0 No. 45017 on 18 July 1967. The Furness Fells make a splendid backdrop to this fine photograph. (*Ken Hale*)

Above and opposite: An interesting trio of pictures, all taken within a few minutes of each other on Grayrigg bank on 17 September 1966. The first shows ex-LMS Class 8F 2–8–0 No. 48186 toiling up the heavy grade with a northbound freight train. A few minutes later, a Crewe–Carlisle freight appears, hauled by 'Black Five' 4–6–0 No. 44765 (off Crewe South shed – 5B). As was often the practice on this steep bank (6 miles of around 1 in 106 to 131), the heavier goods trains had banking assistance, in this case by ex-LMS Fairburn 2–6–4 tank No. 42251, shedded at Tebay (12E). These shots give some idea of the steam traffic that could still be seen in this area in 1966/67.

Above and opposite, top: After Grayrigg bank, the WCML runs for 6 miles on comparatively level track, running through Low Gill and Dillicar in the beautiful Lune Valley, before reaching Tebay and the start of the 5 miles of 1 in 75 up to Shap summit. Ex-Crosti Class 9F 2–10–0 No. 92024 has just run through the Lune Valley and is rounding the curve to Low Gill with a heavy mixed southbound freight train on Thursday 15 September 1966. No. 92024 was one of a batch of ten Class 9Fs (Nos 92020–9) fitted with a Crosti boiler. Later, the Crosti pre-heater was sealed off and the locomotive worked normally. On the same day and a few minutes later at the same location, Class 5MT 4–6–0 No. 45025 approaches the curve to Dillicar with a northbound goods. Just below the white house on the right-hand side was where the line from Clapham (see page 123) came in to join the WCML. To the left of the picture is now the M6 motorway, which at this point follows the curve of the railway.

'Britannia' Pacific No. 70011 *Hotspur* runs through the Lune Valley on 22 July 1967 with an Up freight. Steam workings finished on the Carnforth–Carlisle section of the WCML at the end of 1967. (*John Cooper-Smith*)

Heading north through the Lune Valley, we come to Dillicar water troughs, sited just south of Tebay station. Class 5MT 4–6–0 No. 45094 heads a lengthy Down goods over the troughs on the morning of Saturday 25 June 1966. The lane in the background has been somewhat enlarged, and is now the M6 motorway!

A smart-looking van train pulls out of Tebay on 13 September 1966 with 4–6–0 No. 44911 in charge, and crosses the River Lune just south of the station. On the loop line is a northbound freight awaiting banking assistance. Tebay MPD, home to the Shap bankers, can be seen just to the left of the freight, and straight ahead is the small ex-LNWR station.

At Greenholme, roughly halfway up the 6 miles of Shap bank, Class 5MT 4–6–0 No. 44878 works hard with a northbound ballast train on 19 July 1967. Banking assistance is provided by BR Standard Class 4MT 4–6–0 No. 75029. (*John Cooper-Smith*)

There used to be a saying 'It always rains at Shap!' It may not always have been true, but on several visits to the Scout Green area in 1966 and 1967, if not raining, it was often dull weather. However, the sight of steam at work on this notorious incline more than made up for the vagaries of the Westmorland weather. On 30 August 1967, 'Britannia' Pacific No. 70035 *Rudyard Kipling* pauses just below Scout Green signal-box for a much-needed 'blow-up'. The banker is Standard Class 4MT 4–6-0 No. 75037. On the late morning of 25 June 1966 (see the photograph on page 132 for a contrast in weather conditions on the same day), Class 5MT 4–6–0 No. 44767 approaches Scout Green in fine style with the 09.25 Blackpool–Glasgow train (Saturdays only). An hour or so later, and the bad weather is setting in, as a Glasgow-bound passenger train, hauled by Pacific No. 70041 *Sir John Moore*, climbs the 1 in 75 of Shap near to Scout Green signal-box. Turning round from the previous scenes, and on the same morning, another 'Britannia' Pacific, this time No. 70031 *Byron*, heads downgrade past the LNWR signal-box at Scout Green with the 09.10 Dundee–Blackpool train.

A powerful study of ex-LMS Fairburn 2–6–4 tank No. 42251 as it banks a heavy goods train up the 1 in 75 of Shap incline. The location is near Greenholme, and the date is Saturday 30 July 1966. (*John Cooper-Smith*)

'Britannia' Pacific No. 70004 (formerly *William Shakespeare*) makes a fine sight as it pulls out of Penrith with the 08.00 Carlisle–Birmingham train on 22 July 1967. Dominating the scene is the very high repeating signal. No. 70004 was once the pride of the Southern Railway, being shedded at Stewarts Lane (75D), and would often work the prestigious 'Golden Arrow' and other boat trains. Its final shed was Carlisle Kingmoor (12A), and it was withdrawn from traffic in December 1967. (*Ken Hale*)

An exciting scene at Plumpton, just north of Penrith, on 4 November 1967, as 4–6–2 No. 70021 *Morning Star* speeds south with the 08.05 Carlisle to Redbank (Manchester) parcels train, and passes 'Black Five' No. 45013 waiting to leave the goods loop with the 07.10 Carlisle–Banbury goods train. Note the use of a telephoto lens, at that time a comparatively new innovation in railway photography. (*Ken Hale*)

These two shots at Carlisle station were taken on Wednesday 30 March 1966 and show, first of all, Class 5MT No. 44854 waiting to leave with the 16.37 service to Bradford (via the S&C route) with, in the distance, ex-Ivatt Class 2MT 2–6–2 tank No. 41217 shunting vans. The second shows another Class 2MT 2–6–2 tank, No. 41285, also engaged on shunting duties. Note the fine station outer wall, which at one time was fixed to an equally fine overall roof in Victorian Gothic style, which was replaced in the late 1940s by a smaller and more 'modern' design.

Above and opposite: The next two pictures were taken at one of the last MPDs to close, Rose Grove shed (10F), Burnley, on 19 July 1968, just a few days before closure and the end of BR steam. The first scene shows Class 8F 2–8–0 No. 48723 at the ash pits. In the second, several by now redundant 'Black Five' 4–6–0s and Class 8F 2–8–0s cluster round the vacuum-powered turntable.

On Sunday 4 August 1968, several special steam charter trains were run in the North-West by railway societies to commemorate the end of BR steam. One of the two specials run by the Stephenson Locomotive Society (SLS) is seen passing Hoddlesden Junction, near Darwen, hauled by 'Black Five' 4–6–0s Nos 44874 and 45017, on its outward journey to Blackburn. (*Hugh Ballantyne*)

Opposite: These two photographs show the BR '15 Guinea Special' on Sunday 11 August 1968. The first section of the special from Liverpool Lime Street to Manchester Victoria was hauled by 'Black Five' 4–6–0 No. 45110, seen here pausing appropriately at Rainhill (site of the 1830 locomotive trials) for the hundreds of people who had come along to witness this historic occasion. From Manchester to Carlisle (via the S&C) the train was hauled by the last 'Britannia' Pacific in service, No. 70013 *Oliver Cromwell*. The special is seen approaching Ais Gill summit, where it paused for a photographic stop, much to the delight of the many people who had turned up to see it. In fact, there were so many people at Ais Gill that there was a certain amount of difficulty in re-starting the train.

The final scene shows the return special from Carlisle to Manchester at speed near Helm (on the S&C north of Kirkby Stephen) hauled by Class 5MT 4–6–0s Nos 44871 and 44781. The special was then hauled from Manchester to Liverpool by No. 45110. Adieu steam.